Is Your Life Out of Whack?

Is Your Life Out of Whack?

✦

Methods to restore balance

David Hass

Writer's Showcase
San Jose New York Lincoln Shanghai

Is Your Life Out of Whack?
Methods to restore balance

Writer's Showcase
an imprint of iUniverse, Inc.

For information address:
iUniverse, Inc.
5220 S. 16th St., Suite 200
Lincoln, NE 68512
www.iuniverse.com

Advice based on common sense, not science.

ISBN: 0-595-21804-0

Printed in the United States of America

Contents

Is Your Life Out of Whack?

✦

Methods to restore balance

What is balance? Let's keep this simple. It's more common sense that science.

To my way of thinking there are five factors to keeping your balance: thought, thanks, sleep, food and exercise. There are side issues to each of these keys. We'll discuss those side issues, but please commit those five factors to memory.

They will guide you to creating better balance. Life is a teeter-totter going off-balance on occasion. Maintaining balance requires constant attention.

Just about everything in the world can knock us off balance. Think of things that we encounter daily: a hostile clerk at the convenience store, an angry customer calling on the phone, a fellow employee with a personal problem, etc. The list goes on and on.

And those are just outside influences. On the inside, we get irritated by a family member's actions, the utility bill is higher than expected, our child is ill or having a school problem, the car is acting funny, etc.

And major problems are more common than exceptional: a serious illness, an accident, a divorce, a fire, an injury, etc.

Every one of those situations tips our lives off-balance. We must regain our balance to move forward. Sometimes the world helps us. Sometimes it doesn't.

The purpose of this book is to help you spot off-balance situations and offer suggestions to regain balance.

Even reading this book is only a helping hand. You probably have situations in your life that you sense are causing a loss of balance. Try to find a counter-weight that brings back balance. Remember that thought, thanks, sleep, food and exercise are only my suggested solutions for maintaining balance. You can add or subtract from that formula.

The key is recognizing that balance is essential. You will sense when your life is out of balance. And you are in charge of restoring balance. It's an approach rather than an end.

Is your life balanced? I have to stop and analyze my situation everyday. I usually find that something is off balance. You may see yourself in the chapters that follow. No balance recipe works for everyone. You will have to develop your own using the following suggestions.

GIVE IT SOME THOUGHT

Do you think about things or just react?

More importantly, do you have the time to think about the many aspects of your life? Do you take the appropriate amount of time to consider your options? Do you know what "appropriate amount of time" means?

Today's world is so fast-paced that we have little time to actually sit down and think. The kids are sick so we take them to the doctor. Do we consider that our hectic lifestyles with poor diets, lack of sleep and no "down time" may actually be the cause of family illnesses?

The bills have to be paid on the first of the month so we write the checks or account for our electronic transfers. Do we ever examine ways to cut our bills? Probably not.

We need to slow down this treadmill just a wee bit.

We may not have time to solve world problems, but we can take just a few minutes each day to quietly think.

You might try meditation, reflection or even prayer.

Set aside some time (maybe early in the day) and actually think about your situation in life. You will be surprised how much benefit comes from just a few minutes of thinking. Review the major events of your life: childhood, education, romance, home, family, hobbies, etc.

A short pause in your hectic schedule is likely to give you a positive outlook on life.

BE SURE TO BE THANKFUL

Spirituality has as many different meanings as there are religions. It plays varying roles in the lives of people. One aspect of spirituality—giving thanks—can provide balance to your life.

Giving thanks to God—or at least being appreciative to a Supreme Being—is helpful in maintaining an even keel in daily life. Each day we need to pause for a few moments and give thanks for our blessings. Sometimes that is difficult. A loved one is sick in the hospital, a friend has a death in the family, a parent can't take care of himself or herself, the boss is giving you a hard time, etc.

The list of problems goes on and on.

We need to balance that list. One of the most inspirational groups I know is a national organization called Mended Hearts. The members have all suffered some kind of heart disease problem, usually life-threatening. These people have been at death's door and returned. Many have gone asleep for surgery and wondered if they would ever wake up.

When they do reach the recovery room there is often a newfound appreciation for life. The members of Mended Hearts are thankful to wake up each morning.

We should all be that thankful. Sometimes we can't sleep at night with worry. It's difficult then to be thankful for "little things" like getting out of bed, a cup of coffee or tea and that day's newspaper.

Take time each night—or in the morning if that works better for you—to be thankful. Include on your thankful list a loving family, a roof over your head, food, work, a car, clothes, etc. that allow you to enjoy life. Don't forget your health and a healthy heart.

Being thankful can give you a positive outlook on life. It can balance out those negative factors.

SLEEP FOR THE REST OF YOUR LIFE

Sleep is among the most important factors in achieving balance in our lives. A good night's sleep would make the world a better place. Just think of the increasing number of factors that are competing for our sleep.

More and more households have two wage earners. And often one of those people has a part-time job for extra income. Add family activities such as school, church, exercise, recreation, etc. Then add the usual obligations such as cleaning, yard work, laundry, bill paying, meals, etc. There is little time left for therapeutic sleep.

Tired people are all around us. It would not be surprising if most of the mistakes and accidents in today's world are due to tired and sleepy people. How often have you worked or driven a car when you are tired?

Proper, restful sleep is often neglected. It's my contention that the world would operate more smoothly if not sleep-deprived.

What can you do to achieve sleep balance? First, give sleep a higher priority in your life. Allot enough time (each person has different requirements) for effective and restorative sleep.

"Get tired" before trying to sleep. Physical exercise will contribute to good sleep. Plan to wind down with relaxing activities just before sleeping. Reading is tiring for most people.

Dream before you sleep. Slowly pull yourself out of the day's activities. Visualize a relaxing activity. Pray if you wish. Turn off distractions like the radio, TV and lights.

Restful sleep—at least several nights per week—will help your balance.

EAT RIGHT, EAT LIGHT

Moderation may be the ultimate key to balance. Walk the middle of the road. Don't do anything to excess.

Just about everything in your daily life can be controlled. Too much or too little is the path to avoid. I believe that moderation brings you into balance. You will sense you are doing too much of something or too little. You will feel out of balance.

Did you drink too much wine at the party last weekend? Did you stay up late and not get enough sleep last night? We must avoid those excesses. Moderation is the best policy.

It is especially important when it comes to food. Most of us have eaten too much on occasion. Thanksgiving is the first date that comes to mind. Perhaps you went on a cruise last winter and ate too much for days. You felt uncomfortable and guilty afterward.

My advice is simple: three light meals daily. This is a general guideline. Other ways of eating may work better for you. Three light meals may seem like elementary advice, but try it. You will like it. It's harder than you think.

Eating three meals will be more of a challenge than you think. There is always the temptation to skip breakfast or lunch. That usually leads to a bag of chips or a candy bar for a snack. And that may work for some people, but try to take a few minutes and sit down for three light meals.

I will leave the nutritional balance to dieticians, but I merely say try three light meals. You will feel satisfied and energized. You will avoid a large meal and its sluggish after-effects.

Plan your day to include three light meals. And then—in the evening—review your day and see if you stuck with your plan.

EXERCISE SHOULD BE YOUR OPTION

The bookshelves and magazine racks are filled with publications about fitness and exercise. There's information on the Internet and on TV. You cannot avoid being told about the vital role that exercise plays in a healthy and long life.

There is expert advice everywhere you turn.

Let me tell you a personal story to reinforce the value of exercise. I was active in numerous high school sports, such as football, wrestling, baseball, etc. I loved to participate as well as watch college and professional sports. I had some exposure to proper physical training.

I was heavy in high school and gained more weight when I went off to college, where my food intake increased and my physical activity decreased.

About the time of college graduation I had reached 300 pounds on a 5-9 frame. I knew I had to do something.

I was working my first journalism job on a small newspaper in central Wisconsin. I decided I had to exercise more and eat less. That was my simple plan to lose weight. It worked. I didn't go on any special diet or get any physical training plan. Just exercise more and eat less.

My life was way out of balance with my weight and bad eating habits. I felt my exercise options were limited because of my obesity.

I started walking. I was able to walk to the newspaper office on some days and took time to walk every evening.

Those were literally the first steps in bringing balance back into my life with some regular exercise. I eventually lost about 100 pounds and still hover around 200, not as low as I would like, but an improvement.

There are physical trainers and many other people with far more knowledge about exercise than me, but I know the importance of regular exercise.

Your life will feel more balanced when you exercise daily.

USE THE SALAMI APPROACH

Too much work or responsibility can throw our lives out of balance. We may feel overwhelmed and frustrated. We need to shed those feelings of panic.

If your plate is too full with work, home and family matters, you should consider the "salami approach" to problem solving.

Years ago an elderly woman called the newspaper where I worked and complained that her life was too complicated. She had personal difficulties with her health, the nation was observing its Bicentennial birthday and there was talk about switching to the metric system. She was totally confused. She wanted direction. She was lost. I told her to take one step at a time and not worry about personal and national problems at the same time.

Her case was a strange example, but many people today are similarly overwhelmed by domestic troubles, technology and even using a phone answering machine. The advent of the personal computer is causing headaches for millions of people.

Don't try to eat the entire salami. Cut off one slice and tackle one problem at a time.

The "salami approach" works especially well if you are dealing with complicated material or you have to juggle numerous problems at home and at work. When the challenges are mounting, cut them down to size. Take one problem and work on a solution. Then move to another problem.

Few people have the capacity to solve multiple problems simultaneously.

The "salami approach" works. It reduces your stress and allows you to focus on a single situation with your best effort.

MAKE SOME LISTS

Making written and mental lists can help you focus. Some days the onslaught of daily obligations and problems gets confusing. Our minds get out of balance.

We need to organize our thoughts, goals and chores. We have trouble sorting things out. One thing that works for me is to make lists—both written and mental. There is probably some psychological reason for this, but I attribute this approach—as others in this book—to common sense, rather than science.

I have always made lists, but their importance and necessity became more obvious during my divorce. I put my personal problems on a list, as well as all of the tasks that I faced. I had to move to a different town, stock an apartment, trade in my old car, etc. My plate was full and some days I was both depressed and overwhelmed.

I started making lists. That worked for me. I wrote chores (call utilities, new checking account, etc.) on a legal pad and began crossing them off. I could see where I needed to go and gradually I made progress.

In my mind, I also made lists. What was my focus (my newspaper writing, find a part-time job, etc.)? What were my goals (more income, lose weight, etc.)? What did I want to accomplish each day (thought, thanks, good sleep, three light meals, exercise)? You get the idea.

I carried my written lists under my arm and my mental lists in my brain. Each day I worked on crossing off projects on the written list. Each evening I would mentally review the lists in my head. I felt organized and focused. I felt these lists restored balance.

Lists can also help you. Start with small ones and add. They work.

CUT OUT THE CLUTTER

Simplify. That single word can help you bring balance into your life. Most of the time, life is too complicated.

Are you trying to do too much? You have to be the judge of that, but many of us attempt to accomplish more than we should.

For example, are you trying to raise children (or send them to college), work a job or two, keep romance in your marriage, keep communication open with family and friends, exercise and even more?

Today's economic reality forces most households to seek two incomes. Both spouses work, or one might work two jobs.

I know of a single woman, for example, who works a full-time day job, tends bar two or three nights per week, helps her family with household chores like painting on weekends and still tries to have a social life. That's a plateful. You have to wonder when she sleeps. She, like millions of other people, needs extra income beyond a full-time job, just to make ends meet.

That's the dilemma facing many of us: one salary isn't enough.

Perhaps we can't get by without that part-time job, but then we need to reduce our other obligations. We need to cut down our workload to keep some semblance of balance in our lives. Be selfish—simply take it easy when you aren't working.

CONTROL YOUR CALLS

The telephone can throw us off balance. It's hard to believe that small device has such a powerful attraction. Most of us can't resist a ringing telephone.

No matter what we are doing, we will stop and pick us a ringing phone. Clerks in stores leave a long line of waiting customers to answer the phone. We rush out of the shower with wet hair to answer the phone. We have a full desk of work at the office, but we answer every call—no matter how inconsequential—and interrupt our workflow.

A ringing phone is hypnotic. It pulls us in like a giant magnet.

The answering machine has helped fill a void. We feel better because our phone machine is there to answer when we are not. Does anybody not check their answering machine when they first arrive at home?

The trouble with this phenomenon is that the telephone is too powerful.

We don't have to answer every call. When was the last time you missed a call that impacted your life? Probably never. If a call is important, the person will call back.

Balance is achieved when we set a course of action and then follow through. A ringing telephone throws us off course. It pulls our mind away from our goal and pushes it in a different direction.

It is hard to ignore a ringing telephone the first time, but it gets easier. It gives you a feeling of control to let the phone ring and continue your work. Many people have caller ID or answering machines so nothing is lost by not picking up the telephone. And cellular phones have only added to this phone phenomon.

SKIP SOME MEETINGS

The world revolves around meetings. Too often they are just wastes of time. How do you fight that, especially when your boss has called the meeting? Sometimes there is simply nothing you can do, other times there are courses of action you can take.

The old saying is that the only thing accomplished at most meetings is to call another meeting. Meetings are havens for lazy people who have nothing to do. You need to have a plan for meetings if they are disrupting your day.

I have worked for bosses who routinely held two- or three-hour meetings. One held a series of "get to know you" sessions when he arrived and mine lasted five hours. He did all the talking and I realized afterward that I had a problem on my hands.

There are a couple of things you can do to avoid meetings or keep them moving. If you are in a position to call meetings, make an agenda and set a time limit. Make sure your meetings are concise and meaningful, or cancel them.

If you have too many meetings disrupting the balance of your day, you will have to take action. Start saying no to meetings or have good reasons for conflicts that prevent you from attending a meeting.

One of the best alternatives is to leave early. If no one sets a time limit, set your own. That may even work with the boss. Give an hour to the meeting. Then get up when conversation allows and whisper to someone that you have to take a call. It's a good out and most times people will remember you attended the meeting and will forget that you left early.

Another good option for non-productive meetings is to get paged or get called to the phone. Plan ahead. Arrange for a fellow worker to call you about one hour after the meeting has started. It's a good out.

Manage your meetings. They aren't all bad, but few accomplish very much.

GET A BETTER PERSPECTIVE

It's hard to keep things in perspective. We are too close to our personal problems to see the big picture. Little things—like a driver who cuts you off at the intersection—can be upsetting. Sometimes we let those small things ruin our entire day or more.

A series of disturbing events, even though minor, can route your mental outlook into the dumpster. We must fight back and regain our balance.

Sometimes it is just a matter of refocusing. One suggestion I make is to remember that this is a big world and usually our challenges are small and inconsequential. For example, you have to make a speech and that makes you nervous and uncomfortable. What happens if the worst occurs and your presentation isn't very good? Probably nothing. It will be forgotten in a short time. Will anyone in Spain, Africa or other parts of the world care if you are not a good public speaker?

Another method for you to get a new look on life is to visit some place that is very busy.

For example, drive to a shopping mall and get a cup of coffee. Find a good observation point and just sit down and watch the people. Think of the assortment of problems being shouldered by each of those passers-by. Many of those people probably have worse trouble than you. It gives you perspective to see other people and realize that they also have difficulties.

An airport is a great window to the world. I live near Chicago's O'Hare and Midway airports. Those are fantastic places to observe a parade of people and each of those travelers—you can be assured—has some kind of troubling thought swirling through their minds.

Find some busy public place—a coffee shop inside a discount department store will do—and just watch the world walk by.

GETTING DIRTY ISN'T BAD

We come from the Earth and we go back to the Earth. In between, we don't have much contact with the Earth. A friend of mine once advised me that it is important to get your hands dirty.

This woman believed in reading the alignment of the stars and acting accordingly. She felt the power of crystals taken from the Earth. Her home was filled with rocks and gems. She believed we needed to be closer to the natural elements.

She was a strong person with great patience and faith. I've never been a person who enjoys tending flowers or growing a garden, but I recognize the need to touch the Earth and feel its power. I suggest this is part of keeping our balance.

We need to be in touch with the natural—and powerful—elements of the Earth. It might be something as simple as pulling weeds or as elaborate as planting a large flower or vegetable garden.

See if you don't feel the energy of the Earth when you dig your fingers into the soil and get some dirt under your fingernails.

It's a strange feeling, but it's a force worth feeling.

YOU MUST HAVE HEROES

We need people to emulate. We need heroes. They help us set goals and strive to do better.

We all have our own special interests so the people who you admire will be different than mine.

People in the public eye are usually our role models, but our heroes may live in the same town, they may work where we work or they may be in our own families.

Parents, brothers or sisters may be our heroes. We have different reasons for identifying them as heroes, but usually they set an example for us to follow.

Some of my heroes are in sports. Not necessarily because they are so successful, but primarily because they set good examples in their personal lives and ultimately were successful.

I grew up near Green Bay, Wisconsin when the Packers football team was winning championships. You might expect my football hero to be a player like Bart Starr, but Coach Vince Lombardi is one of my most admired people. Lombardi believed in hard work, discipline and dedication. Those considerations served him well and made him successful.

I think of other sports heroes like golfers Gene Sarazan, Byron Nelson and Jack Nicklaus, who were gentlemen competitors, but also among the best in their business.

Having heroes can inspire you. I think of religious leaders, business people and teachers. Heroes help you set goals and give you guideposts to attain those goals. They might also serve as mentors, but that is a topic of another chapter.

CLEAN HANDS ARE HAPPY HANDS

There are multiple benefits to clean hands.

That may sound funny to you, but take my word that the simple act of washing your hands is good for your sanitary AND emotional health.

First, it gets rid of dirt and the germs. You see signs in rest rooms everywhere: "Wash your hands before returning to work." That's intended for workers, but it's good advice for customers using those rest rooms, as well.

I have written newspaper columns about this subject and the reader response is always positive. My theme is "clean hands are happy hands." After a recent column on this subject, I received a call from a reader backing me and suggesting another step. He said I should do another column advocating that all rest rooms doors swing out so you don't have to touch the handle when you leave.

That's another great idea. I'm no architect, but doors that swing out would allow you to exit without touching the dirty handle. It's great to have soap and hot water to wash your hands in a rest room, but many people don't bother at all. And you grab the handle right after them.

It's my contention that washing your hands can also have an emotional benefit. Years ago I attended a seminar on removing stress from your body. One technique is to do some physical act like washing your hands and imagine the stress draining out of your body. It works for me. I used to work on the news desk with highly stressful deadlines. After the paper was out I would go into the rest room and literally wash my hands of all of that day's difficulties. I would wash the stress right down the drain.

It may work for you. Wash your hands to remove germs and reduce stress. Clean hands are happy hands.

GUARD AGAINST GRUMPINESS

Do people get more cynical as they age? Do they go sour on the world? Why are so many old people grumpy?

Hanging around with grumpy people can rub off. And who wants to be around people who take a dim view of everything?

You probably have some of these people in your life. I know I do. I think we will be talking about this a lot more in the years ahead as the Baby Boomers get older.

Grumpy people often have nothing to be sour about. I have known several older people who have nice homes, excellent health, prosperity and good families. Yet, they possess a very negative outlook.

There is probably some psychological explanation for this, but the intent of this book is to recognize that kind of attitude and avoid it.

I think of one man who was a retired independent businessman. He raised an educated family, he had wealth and independence. Yet he was bitter on the world. He'd be hostile to service people, wouldn't leave a decent tip at a restaurant, had a bad temper, was very opinionated and generally hard to deal with. He had no reason to be grumpy, but he was.

I know of another successful homebuilder who was running a very lucrative business well into his sixties. He loved cars and had a dozen or more. He enjoyed history and indulged that interest with extensive travel. One day he told me that he had to fight being grumpy. He knew the world had treated him well, yet he would get upset and angry about things of little consequence. He said his wife was good about bringing him back in line. He would get all fired up about something that meant little or nothing. His wife would see that and bring him back into balance by reminding him of his substantial lot in life.

The CEO of a large newspaper business told me the same thing. We were talking one day and an elderly man interrupted our conversation with an inconsequential compliant. The CEO said he sees that more and more. And he was concerned that he was getting that way.

Some people have reasons to be unhappy. Sometimes life can knock us out of whack. We have to look at the big picture. Generally we will see that—on average—life has been good to us.

We have no reason to be grumpy.

SPEND TIME WITH KIDS

Sometimes we need a change of mental "scenery." We are stuck in the same rut as everyone else at work. The people in our social and religious circles talk about the same things. We simply spend too much time with adults.

Try hanging around with some kids to get a fresh look at life.

Parents of young children know about this experience. The candor of kids is refreshing. It also puts our problems in perspective.

Not long ago I spent several days with the grandchildren of my sister in another city. They are just at the age of talking. Their comments and viewpoints are amazing.

I normally spend all of my time with adults, either at work or at play. They have mature outlooks, based on considerable experience in work or worldly situations.

My time with these grandchildren was mind-expanding. They found simple pleasures in word games and songs. Kids are generally trusting and wise beyond their years. It's fun to watch kids run and play. Their enthusiasm is contagious.

If your life seems out of whack, spend a little time with kids. They will help you see the world through new eyes.

DON'T BE WASTEFUL

Recycling can bring some balance into your life. There is a feeling of contributing to the preservation of the Earth when you recycle. That's not always possible, but recycling is now available in many communities, where curbside collections include glass, paper, etc.

A good feeling comes when you give back some part of a product after you have used it. There is strong satisfaction from not being wasteful.

It's my belief that our communities get out of whack when they constantly build new structures. People like new buildings, but there's an unsettling feeling when we keep razing old structures and erecting new.

Not long ago I visited Denver, Colorado and observed the successful "recycling" of countless old buildings in that town's Lower Downtown—or LODO—district. A new baseball stadium was constructed nearby, but its façade fits in nicely with the nearby buildings that have been rehabbed.

There is a good feeling from seeing old warehouses remodeled into living spaces and retail establishments. There's a sense that the work of the past was not wasted. A lot of work goes into updating old structures, but there is definitely a comfortable feeling in being in a building that has found a new use.

Tearing down the old without regard for its potential is upsetting to our nature. Recycling—whether a soft drink bottle or an old structure—restores some balance.

LEARN FROM OLD PEOPLE

Your parents always get wiser as YOU age.

The transformation from youth to adulthood is amazing. Children often see their parents as out of touch, unreasonable and lacking wisdom. As the kids grow older, their views of their parents also evolve. The perception is that their parents get smarter. We look in our "personal rear view mirrors" and we see the brilliance of our parents.

It's the same with other people older than us. We know them through work, community, religious and social connections.

When our lives are out of whack, these folks can provide a stabilizing comment or piece of advice.

I mentioned before in this book that there is value in hanging around with children; it works the same way with senior citizens. Their experience can be tapped and valuable lessons learned…all for free, or at least the cost of a cup of coffee or lunch.

Pick out a senior citizen and call them to chat. It's amazing what you can learn. They actually have gotten wiser while YOU aged.

WATER IS RESTORATIVE

There is something very therapeutic about water.

Water is soothing for the soul and psyche. I believe it can bring you back from the edge of frustration.

People who are fortunate to live near a large body of water may not receive the same benefit. I grew up living along a small river in central Wisconsin. The flow of the Wolf River provided that calming effect, but not like a large lake or an ocean.

The water is refreshing without taking a drink.

If your personal situation is unnerving, try a getaway—short or long—at the water's edge. I have found that works for me. I now live in a condo next to a small lake and it is very relaxing in the evening to watch the sunset.

It's great if you can afford a cottage or weekend home, but even a brief visit can provide some relief. Try renting a cottage, condo or even hotel room close to the water.

Rivers and lakes offer tremendous recreation, but just being close has a calming effect. Try drinking your morning coffee, tea or juice on a quiet dock. Or have the evening snack or cocktail at the waterfront restaurant. The ocean tides are ideal, but even an inland lake can bring some relaxation.

My current home is near Chicago and Lake Michigan. The beauty of that body of water can bring you peace and provide quiet reflection. I believe it can work for you.

RECOGNIZE OUR ABUNDANCE

Our food stores are jammed on weekends. The days before holidays—especially Thanksgiving—are hectic in the aisles of supermarkets.

Shoppers are loading their grocery carts with all kinds of meats, vegetables, fruits, canned goods and household products.

The abundance and selection of fresh food is absolutely amazing in the grocery store right down the streets from our homes.

We take that for granted.

Even items such as out-of-season fruits and vegetables are on the shelves if we want to pay a premium price.

When your life gets wacky it can be refreshing just to walk through a supermarket—not necessarily to buy—but to just marvel at the harvest of this great nation. Think of how many millions of other people on this Earth are not as fortunate. Think how our ancestors would be astounded to see food items on the shelves from all over the world.

Food takes center stage during holidays and special celebrations, but we have many reasons to give thanks every day for the bounty that is available at our fingertips.

SAVOR EVERY SWALLOW

Sometimes we just need to slow down to enjoy life's simple pleasures.

Eating is a good example.

We have been told that breakfast is a very important meal to start the day, yet we rush to get in a few bites before bolting out of the door for work or school.

At mid-day we drive through the carry-out lane at the fast food restaurant so we can eat in the car and still run a few errands before heading back to work.

The evening meal is not much better. There are few occasions when we actually sit down and slowly eat our dinner.

Our "to do" list is long. And slowly eating meals is not on that list.

I'm as guilty as anyone, but every so often I remember that rushing around and eating hastily is knocking balance out of my life. I geared down one morning recently and pictured the foods I was eating. I enjoyed potatoes from Idaho, mushrooms and peppers with my eggs from Wisconsin and orange juice from Florida. It was a feast for the senses.

Eating is a simple pleasure that can be enhanced by slowly chewing and pausing. You won't take time to do this for every meal, but try it on occasion.

A NEIGHBORHOOD IS CALMING

Even driving to work or home can make you frazzled. Do you ever feel that way?

You are organized and focused when you leave the house in the morning. You are ready for a productive day at work.

Then wham! Traffic is terrible. Someone cuts you off when it's your turn at the intersection. Pokey drivers and speeders cause irritation.

Your entire frame of mind has changed by the time you get to work.

It happens to all of us. A relaxing trip to work—whether you go a short distance or have a long commute—turns into a nightmare.

I have found the best way to avoid this is to take the long way to work and drive slowly through the neighborhoods. It takes just a little more time, but it's not as taxing on your state of mind.

Residential neighborhoods are peaceful compared to the congested arteries that we usually travel. It will take a few minutes longer, but you won't get upset with discourteous drivers.

It's also a lot more interesting to check out other neighborhoods. You might see a landscaping idea that would work at your home. It's fun to watch the other parts of your community waking up.

You drive slower in someone else's neighborhood, and your mental frame of mind also slows down. You arrive at work without frustration.

CHOOSE YOUR NEWS CAREFULLY

The daily news is depressing. I always tell my wife that I don't want to listen to the 10 p.m. news because it contains so much bad news, and right before we fall asleep. Sunday night news in the summer is the worst. For example, a family gathering is shattered when a youngster drowns. A weekend retreat is ruined by a boating accident and on and on.

I worked for a community newspaper and here I am telling you to be careful about how much news you digest.

To me there is a vast difference between the "cool" approach of reading a newspaper and the "hot" approach of listening to the radio or watching TV. The electronic media is much more sensational and you have to sit and watch or listen. You don't have to read the entire story in a newspaper. You can turn the page or just put down the newspaper.

In fact, I would advocate just scanning the headlines. Generally, there is more positive news than negative, but the bad stuff gets all of the big headlines. You can separate the good news by just being careful what you read.

In addition, it has been my experience in the news business to never advocate ignoring the news. You won't fall behind by skipping news from around the world, but you will get short-changed avoiding the local news. You might miss the death of an acquaintance, a ticket announcement for a special event or just a sale at the local store.

I have had far too many people call me asking about a news story that has already been in the paper.

My advice is to scan. Sift and winnow. Be selective about how you obtain news. Keep track of news that is important to you and avoid the rest.

A HANDSHAKE SAYS A LOT

There are telltale signs that someone's life may be out of whack. Those indications are not foolproof, but they give you an inkling.

One sign that reveals strength or instability is the handshake.

How many times have you reached out to someone expecting a firm grip and instead received a limp rag?

People with confidence and balance in their lives have a strong, arm-pumping handshake.

You can fool people about your personal situation with a good handshake, but in general a good grip is a good overall sign.

You have to be careful with those handshakes. I advise firm, but not a vise.

Be sincere, but don't squeeze too much. When your life is sailing along it will show in your handshake. Let people know you are in control and your life is in balance.

MAKE THIS DAY YOUR LAST DAY

Treat every day like it's your last. This may be the most important bit of advice in this book.

Think how you would want to spend tomorrow if it was going to be your last day.

What would you do? What would you say? Who would you want to be with?

We often lose sight of how lucky we are to be alive. Maybe it's a bad day at work or some kind of a problem at home. There's a death in the family, an argument with your mate or something happens that is upsetting.

Your life is knocked out of whack. This little mental exercise can bring you right back into balance: Pretend this is your last day. You will appreciate everything a lot more. Your distress, frustration and anger will subside. The cloud over your head will disappear.

You will see that most situations are inconsequential. They are not important to your overall well-being. You will be able to see the important things in life are faith, health, family and friends. The material things that often are behind your trouble are not important at all.

Treat every day like it's your last.

GIVE AND YOU WILL RECEIVE

You can never give too much back to the world.

It may surprise you that everyone—rich and poor; with substantial resources or without—is in a position to give back to the world.

We are blessed in differing ways. Some people have wealth. Some people have talent. Some people may have an abundance of time.

Public service—giving back to your community—will bring you more satisfaction than you can imagine.

If you can't afford to donate financially, donate your time as a volunteer.

Countless organizations are looking for volunteers. Check your local newspapers, call your United Way office or check at your neighborhood church or school if you need some direction.

One of my favorite places needing volunteers is the local animal shelter. I have written animal shelter newspaper columns for years and every shelter needs helping hands.

It's great therapy for young and old. Dogs and cats need grooming. Kennels need cleaning. Often, the animals just need attention. You will be amazed at how good you feel when just a little attention caused a puppy to wag his tail or a kitten to purr.

This is a giving nation. You just have to find the right way to contribute. You will get far more in return than you can ever give.

HAND OUT SELF-ESTEEM

One effective technique for work managers is to create self-esteem in employees.

It also works in situations away from the work place.

It goes something like this: A manager has an employee who generally does a good job, but often is late for work. The boss calls in the worker and says, "You are a valued employee who works hard and always gets the job done. You need to apply that same commitment to arriving at work on time…"

You get the idea. Say something positive and then get your point across. It's the adage that a little bit of sugar makes the medicine go down easier.

Try that philosophy in your daily living. To the waitress: "you are such an excellent server; do customers ever suggest that you wash your hands since you handle money?"

To the convenient store clerk: "You have such a great attitude; has your boss ever offered some training in counting change?"

One goal could be to correct a day-to-day irksome situation that is causing you consternation. Don't procrastinate. Try this corrective measure. If it doesn't work, go to other places of business. Your daily routine needs to be in balance most of the time to be effective and happy.

If that is not the case, you need to make changes.

GIVE A HUG, TAKE A HUG

There's something especially good about physical contact. A friend of mine—a member of the clergy—used to hug every person he met, acquaintance or stranger. The latter often hugged cautiously or with startled looks.

This minister believed a hug was better than a mere greeting or even a handshake.

I agree. It's easier for me to hug females than males, but that's probably just some old psychological hang-up.

An embrace sends a strong message that you are in touch with the other person. That full-body gesture also helps you keep your mental balance. It only lasts a few seconds, but a hug is energy—and strength—sharing. You physically transmit your friendship and feeling toward the other human being.

You have to be brave to hug all of the people you meet. Some will not feel comfortable with a hug. The physical contact, however, will help if your life feels out of whack.

NOTICE BEAUTY

Notice the beautiful things in this world that God and man have created.

A stream running in the mountains; A tree whose leaves have turned golden as winter approaches; A clear sky. These are just a handful of nature's amazing creations.

I don't think anyone can match the beauty of a simple flower—even a dandelion—but man has done some marvelous things. Just pausing to behold that beauty can help bring your life back into balance. The architecture of an old building, the brush strokes on a painting, and even the engineering in a finely crafted automobile are astonishing.

There is so much to appreciate in this world.

We have world-class art museums in many cities, but even walking down an elementary school's hallways and seeing what children have created is awe-inspiring.

I get great satisfaction golfing on a course that was designed with consideration for nature. I'm not a great golfer, but I love the scenery and serenity of a beautiful golf course.

A walk in the park or even borrowing an art book from the library can lift your spirit. There's beauty all around. Just look for it.

TAKE A NEW SEAT

It's my contention that adding some variety to your life also adds some balance. Some changes—even minor ones like driving to work on a different route—can help you gain a new perspective.

Most of us are proverbial creatures of habit.

I think that's good on most counts since a certain amount of routine helps you get a lot accomplished. Routine helps you eliminate some decisions on mundane matters, like the best way for you to get ready for work in the morning.

It's good, however, to shake things up once in awhile. I'm not talking about wholesale changes on a regular basis, just adding some occasional variety.

A few years ago I wrote a column for my newspaper about sitting in different seats during a given week.

For example, do you always sit in the same chair when you watch TV, eat in the dining room or at the kitchen table?

Do you always grab the same spot when there is a meeting at work? Or take the same seat on the commuter train?

Do you always sit in the same pew at your church or synagogue?

Try sitting someplace else. It might provide the variety you need to spark some vitality or enthusiasm.

Changing seats will surprise others. You will see them—and they will see you - from a different angle.

You will be pleased with the results. You might find that a new chair gives you a better view of the outdoors. It may demonstrate to your boss and others around you that you have a creative streak.

Try sitting in a new spot. If you don't like it, you can always move back.

"ABSORB" NEW NAMES

Feeling unsure of yourself can knock your attitude out of whack, at least temporarily.

A sense of confidence comes from being in control of most situations. Do you ever feel awkward or uneasy in business or social situations when you meet new people?

Do you have trouble remembering their names?

That happens to me all the time. I'm introduced to a new couple, but I fail to retain either one or both of their names.

That makes me feel awkward. I'm trying to recall a name and talking at the same time.

We get those feelings of anxiety.

It takes a little concentration and some practice to get better at name retention. Perhaps you have heard the tip to associate someone else's name with some other object or person. For example, when you meet an "Art," think of Art Garfunkel to remember Art's name. That works.

The other advice I use is to slow down and ask to have the new person's name repeated. Then I repeat the other person's name out loud. It helps. A little repetition helps you remember names.

My suspicion is that we generally are trying to move too quickly. We are in a room full of people and we don't take the time to absorb the names of people we meet.

Gear down. Meet only a few people and remember their names. It's a good habit and keeps your attitude from going out of whack.

Mentally tell yourself to use this technique at work and in social situations. You will have to practice to get better, but it will work.

REHEARSE FOR PARTIES

Social situations can make some people feel uncomfortable. They are not sure what to talk about and that makes them feel awkward.

Other people are chatterboxes and never stop talking. They can skip this chapter. They don't need advice on handling receptions, parties, open houses, etc.

One of the best ways I have discovered to handle social situations is to practice ahead of time. That's right: practice for parties.

Some people retain a lot of information about social acquaintances. They remember the names of their family members, special interests, hobbies, etc. Others—like me, and possibly you—don't remember all of that personal data. (We're not talking about close friends or relatives here, but rather people who you only see on occasion.)

For those people you only meet periodically, it's good to make some mental notes at first and then later make some written notes. It's a great way to remember more about people. I know this worked for me in one neighborhood where I lived. I would only talk with the neighbors once or twice a year (usually a Christmas party). From year to year, I would forget some bits of personal information.

I solved this problem by jotting down some personal facts on each family after one Christmas party. The next year I pulled out those notes and refreshed my memory.

I could ask about one neighbor's son in college, another person's interest in collecting model trains or another's volunteer work with the church.

I was prepared to meet the neighbors and I felt better about this social situation. I retained much more personal information and I'm sure they felt better, too.

I had "rehearsed" for a party.

It will work for you. You will be able to talk freely and ask questions. You won't stand there thinking: "I can't remember that guy's name and I'm too embarrassed to ask again."

This little tip will make you feel much more at ease in social situations. You will need to update this information after each party, but it's surprising how much more you retain when you write it down.

USE MAPS TO FANTISIZE

We all need a little fantasy in our lives. One of the best—and safest—ways that I have found is to pick up a map.

A world map is great, but a road atlas of the United States or even the state highway map in the glove compartment of your car will do.

If you are having a bad day, just open up one of those maps and look at all of the different towns. It will take your mind off of your troubles.

Looking at a map is a great way to daydream.

It doesn't cost anything. It's convenient and it moves your thoughts away from any troubles you are experiencing.

A map gives you perspective and opens your eyes to other possibilities.

Think about life in New York City or some small town in Montana.

Imagine what it's like today in London or Cairo, Egypt.

Find the towns where your relatives live and consider what they are doing today.

Dream about a vacation.

A map won't cure all of your ills, but it may give you some direction to escape your present troubles.

MEMORY AIDES

Forgetting things is a major source of frustration.

Old people berate themselves for loss of memory. They shake their heads when they can't remember why they walked from one room to another. These seniors forget that malady afflicts young people as well. Kids forget as much as the elderly, but they don't blame that deficiency on aging. They just blow it off.

Nothing is worse than forgetting something important. We get thoughts and they disappear. That happens in the shower, driving the car and just gazing out of the window.

My remedy is to carry 3 by 5 note cards and a pen. Jot down anything you want to remember. Don't wait very long to do that or the idea will pass.

I have used this suggestion successfully for years. I didn't realize how many others used it until one day I was working out at the local heath club. The Congressman who represents our district was on the treadmill next to me. We have known each other professionally for years. That day we were just chatting.

I mentioned something about an upcoming column that I had written. He reached into a pocket, took out a blank card and wrote down a note. "I'd be lost without these," he smiled.

I agree. Simple note cards will ease the frustration of forgetting important thoughts. That is, if you remember to use them.

DON'T WAIT

Hesitation causes trepidation. Don't wait.

Most of us—me included—are prone to over-analyze. We weigh the pros and cons before making a decision. That's not always bad, but often our first inclination is our best inclination. It's like answering a multiple-choice question: If we read the choices long enough, they all start to look correct.

A very successful businessman told me long ago to "go with your gut reaction." That's a good philosophy to follow. It won't always work, but it will be right most of the time.

This businessman was nearly bankrupt less than a decade ago. He caught a few breaks in the business world, he went with his "gut reaction" and now he's sailing along.

This advice doesn't mean, however, to ignore looking at all options carefully. Just don't over do it.

A young man I know has talent in many areas. He's in sales, but he gets bored easily. He's constantly talking about changing jobs, but he can't "pull the trigger" and make a change. I have suggested to him to give something else a whirl. If it doesn't work, he can always switch again.

Most of us are similar to this young man. We are reluctant to change. I think it's a good idea to try other things even if they don't work out. You learn from mistakes. Don't hesitate.

BECOME AN ALMANAC AFFICIONADO

What's your favorite book? Is it a mystery? A biography?

The Bible, of course, is the perennial best seller. It sits on more nightstands than any other book for those quiet moments just before falling asleep.

People have asked me about my favorite book and I always reply, "the world almanac."

There's a new version published each year and many varieties are on the shelves of your favorite bookstore. If you decide to buy one, just flip through one and see if it strikes your fancy. I can't make a specific recommendation because so many fit the bill.

I do suggest that you have a current world almanac in your home.

It will settle countless arguments, provide valuable information on a long list of subjects and serve as an up-to-date resource for projects at home, work or in school. You will be shocked at the wealth of information in those tomes if you are not already an almanac afficionado.

The world almanac is my favorite book. Don't be at home (or at work) without it.

Just page through an almanac and you will be impressed. It's a condensed encyclopedia.

They are inexpensive and make great gifts.

This unique information source will answer many of your questions and help you feel comfortable and more confident.

LET COMPLIMENTS SOAK IN

Let some things soak in.

People are in such a rush today that they are becoming immune to both complaints and compliments. That's how we are trained to operate. People who deal with the public find they can't handle the stress if they allow customer comments to upset them.

In my work as a writer of opinion columns for a newspaper, I have dealt with many controversial issues. I have expressed my opinion on countless subjects. I get some positive feedback, but many people call or write with strong, opposing views. Sometimes they want to argue and persuade me to change the position that I expressed in the newspaper. That doesn't happen very often.

It's similar to most jobs that deal with customer service, whether you are waiting on tables or working as a telemarketer. Customers have complaints and they want you to satisfy them. That doesn't happen very often.

It's my belief that people are getting "thicker skin."

They have grown that "thicker skin" to cope with criticism. Unfortunately, that protective shell also prevents compliments from soaking in. People treat compliments with the same casual regard. We have to pay attention to these comments, and I encourage people to hear compliments, accept them and let them soak in. We need our self-esteem enhanced.

Don't treat complaints and compliments in the same way. Dismiss complaints that you can't resolve, but allow your brain to absorb kind words.

BE A TURTLE

Be patient. Take small steps.

I think that advice is good in all phases of life. I have always had the feeling that things that come too quickly or too easily simply don't last. Most success must be obtained the old-fashioned way. You have to earn it.

I learned this lesson while training to run a marathon. Preparing to run over 25 miles takes time. It cannot be rushed. It must be done in bits and pieces over a long period.

That approach applies to most worthwhile goals. You need to decide what you want to achieve, lay out a reasonable schedule, follow that schedule and your goal will be attained.

A former advertising colleague of mine always said: "Plan your work; work your plan." I used that philosophy to complete two marathons in Chicago.

Be a turtle.

THE COMFORT OF BOOKS

Don't you feel comfortable just holding this book? There is nothing quite like the permanence and stability you feel from holding (and reading) a book.

Cable TV, personal computers and the Internet are threats to the publishing industry, but I'm not sure the day will ever come that books are replaced by electronic reading. My view, however, might be considered prehistoric in a couple more decades.

I worked for a small newspaper outside of Chicago, but I'm convinced the days of newspapers are numbered. Someday, we will look back and say: "I can't believe they cut down all of those trees to produce newspapers!"

The information age is moving people in all kinds of directions. That can make you feel out of whack, whatever your age. Holding a book, reading it, saving it on your bookshelf at home is one way to regain some balance.

The day is near when large numbers of people will get most of their information on a single screen (TV or computer) in their homes. In fact, the day is already here for some folks. People already have the capability to print out articles (hopefully some of my newspaper columns) that they want to keep. People will also have their own electronic libraries to save information on travel, recipes, etc.

You look around your community at bookstores and can't imagine that the day might come when they won't exist. I hope that's not soon, but I fear the worst.

PULL OUT OF UNHAPPY MUD

Find something to do that you like. In this instance I am specifically thinking about your job, but this applies to other aspects of life as well.

There is so much frustration around us. It's my contention that the major source of unhappiness is that people don't like their jobs. It's as simple as this: people who enjoy their work are happier people.

And a large number of people aren't pleased with their work lives. Very few people say, "I like my job." When I hear that, I say "you must be the only person on Earth who likes his job." It doesn't matter about your income. People who earn large amounts of money and people who earn little all share the same complaint: they don't like their jobs.

If that is your problem, I suggest finding something else to do. That, of course, is easier said than done. You may feel constrained by lack of education, family obligations, age, etc. Try to do something else. Even considering other work options or actually searching for a new job will bring some spark back into your life.

Life is too short to be stuck in the mud of unhappy work.

And if changing is absolutely impossible for you, find something to add to your life to bring you pleasure and take your mind off of work. Find a new hobby, volunteer to help other people, turn your interest in some other direction. Maybe something as simple as spending more time reading will help you.

There are many things (i.e. work, hobbies, community groups) that you will enjoy. Find them.

YOU NEED TO LAUGH

Find out whatever makes you laugh and do that. Do you laugh at TV shows? Do you enjoy hearing comedians? Do you laugh when you read certain writers?

For me, I always get a laugh when reading columns by humorist Dave Barry.

There's probably some psychological reason why laughing is good for us, but suffice to say that it makes you feel good. It takes your mind off of daily troubles.

The world is just too serious. On some days we may be content, but a tragedy in some other part of the nation or world brings us down. That's the way it works with global communications. We have access to information from every part of the world.

The down side is that bad news causes heartache. We literally carry the weight of the world.

Shrug that off. Put a smile on your face and laugh at the world around you.

The big stores have books on comedy, humor and jokes, if you need them. Can't afford to buy a book? Go to the library.

THE STORY OF YOUR LIFE

What is the story of your life? Are you content? Are you doing what you want to do? Do you need to make a change?

You are the author of "The Story of Your Life." Are you "writing" your story in the way you want it written? More importantly, will there be a happy ending to your story?

We have all heard the flip phrase, "That's the story of my life." Those words are usually used to describe bad luck: You miss the winning lottery combination by one number. You hit all red lights when you are in a hurry and all green lights when you are killing time.

"That's the story of my life." You may even use that phrase.

The interesting part is that you can change the story of your life.

Don't accept what is being handed to you. Don't resign yourself to your present condition.

Make some changes. It's not too late to rewrite "the story of your life."

If your story line is not making you happy, then you need to write some new chapters. Think of your life as a book that is still in progress. Change the script. It is the story of your life and no one else.

WORK AT FINDING WORK

For many people their jobs are critical to their well-being. The value that people place on their employment varies, of course, but a paycheck alone is incentive enough to make people pay attention to their jobs.

Sometimes, however, a change needs to be made.

Whatever your reason, you might find yourself in a position of looking for different employment.

That can be an exhilarating experience or it might be a nightmare.

A university professor once told me that the best way to look for work is to consider that task "a regular job."

Get up early in the morning and get ready for work. Start at 8 and don't quit unit 5. In essence: work at getting work.

Many people spend just a little time each day on their job hunt. That's not the best or most productive method.

Make your "job" hunting for a job. Write letters, make calls, hunt through ads, search trade publications, hire an employment agency, use the Internet, network and call potential business contacts. There's a lot you can do to find a job.

Work at finding a new job. It will pay off.

KAY AND WALLY MART

Many newspaper columnists create characters to tell stories to their readers. I remember Slats Grobnik in the late Mike Royko's columns in the Chicago Tribune. One of my colleagues developed a bar buddy called Fats McGillicudy.

These characters talk with the readers and special points are made through their dialogue. I tried the same technique.

I created Kay And Wally Mart. They are just everyday folks who use a lot of common sense. One reader even wrote in and suggested that they name their dog Sport Mart.

We need alter egos.

That is at least part of the motivation for watching TV dramas, sit-coms and soap operas. We identify with the fictional characters and we enjoy their personas. Is that bad? Not in my book. I think relating to fiction—TV, movies, books, etc.—is good for the spirit. It allows us to step out of our world and into someone else's situation. Millions of people do this with daytime TV and prime time shows.

Kay and Wally Mart love these shows and I never argue with them.

CHIVALRY AND CIVILITY

You have probably heard that chivalry is dead. Well, how about civility?

I'm concerned that both of these commendable qualities are being lost in the hectic shuffle of daily life.

They are virtues worth pursuing.

Their demise is a direct result of loss of respect for other people in general. Have you noticed this trend?

Chivalry embodies the traits of courtesy, gallantry and generosity. They are easy to forget when someone is cutting in front of you in the supermarket checkout line.

Civility is defined as politeness. It is easy to forget when you are concerned about road rage on your way to work.

Respect can be cultivated. It can be taught to children. It can be practiced by adults.

We need to revive both chivalry and civility.

Treat other people with respect and your mood—as well as those around you—will be improved.

BE PROUD OF OLD GLORY

People are advised to have love, friendship and concern for others if they want to have fulfilling lives.

Let me add one more ingredient: patriotism.

It's my belief that a love of country and commitment to national goals are important to having a well-rounded and satisfying life.

An understanding of the sacrifices that made this nation creates an appreciation of our freedom.

This is an amazing country based on idealism and concern for others. We must never loose sight of those goals. Many lives have been lost to defend this nation and the freedom of its people.

We need to take pride in our national symbols, such as our flag, Pledge of Allegiance, National Anthem and founding patriots. One of my favorite symbols is the bald eagle. It's not a perfect bird, but to me the eagle stands for strength and soaring spirit.

Be proud when you gaze upon Old Glory. This nation has a rich past and vast potential. This is a great place to live.

CUT LOSSES ON BAD DAYS

Sometimes you just have a bad day.

The stars are aligned against you. The universe won't cooperate. And the car won't start.

You feel like crawling back into bed, but that is rarely an option. You have too many responsibilities at home and work.

You bravely venture out, knowing full well that things aren't going to work out. You have to fight through that.

Your life is out of whack. The stoplights are all red. You spill coffee on your desk at work. You have a bad day at work and one of the kids is sick.

You can't win. The only redeeming thought is that tomorrow is a new day and things will be better. It's astounding that some days are just ill-fated, but we have to live with that.

When you run into a string of failures, recognize that and be careful. Put off some decisions if that is possible. Ride out the storm.

Today's difficult choice is sometimes easier tomorrow.

We all have these trying days. Cut them short, if you can, and retreat to the safety of your home. A good night's sleep and a sunny day may make the murky choice a little clearer.

There will be bad days, but cut your losses and move on.

TRY SOME SILENCE

The noise around us is annoying and distracting. Think of the sounds you hear everyday: Traffic, phones ringing, people talking, kids crying, radios and TVs playing, etc.

Our ears take a beating. They might need a rest.

How often do you sit in a silent home? Probably not very often. Try it. It is so rare that you may even feel uncomfortable in silence. I suggest pulling the plug on all noise—at least occasionally—and let your mind take some time off, free from distractions. You might be surprised. Silence is relaxing and calming.

I worked in a newsroom that was loaded with noise. There was constant conversation. People were talking to each other or to someone on the phone. The police scanner was picking up emergency calls. A phone was always ringing. I became accustomed to that noise over the years. You probably do the same where you work. You just block out the noise.

That's good because it does allow you to work in a noisy environment. When you get home, however, find a quiet spot and soak in the silence. It's refreshing.

EXTEND OLIVE BRANCHES

Following a recent election there was a front-page headline in the newspaper that informed me that the winning state gubernatorial candidate had "extended an olive branch" to the political party he had defeated.

That's good advice for all of us.

The olive branch is a symbol of peace. To me, it also signifies forgiveness and a willingness to cooperate.

Don't let your life get out of whack with too much animosity. Some people carry grudges for years and that hampers or destroys their effectiveness. Let go of hard feelings and hatred. Harboring those emotions won't do you any good.

Sometimes it's hard to forgive and forget, but that is necessary to get on with your life.

We might be tempted to jab our opponents and adversaries with other kinds of sticks, but extending an olive branch is the first step toward healing those rifts and moving on.

MAKE SOME VOCABULARY CHANGES

Exercise and exorcise your vocabulary.

The way we express ourselves is a lasting way to make an impression. People notice and remember certain characteristics—physical and otherwise—about other people. Size, stature, clothes, hair, etc. are just a few tip-offs.

We often work on those features to make improvements. The adage that your first impression is your most important impression still holds.

We shine our shoes, wear appealing clothes and take care of personal hygiene, but generally we neglect our vocabulary.

There have been occasions when another person's means of expression made either a favorable or unfavorable impression. You met a stranger and thought, "that person is bright" or "that person is a dullard."

We pay attention to external details like our hair, but we neglect inner details like our vocabulary.

When I was single, I used to go to a neighborhood pub for pizza or a burger. There was a tall and cute bartender. It was obviously flirting, but I used to say, "Julie, instead of a tip tonight I am going to give you a new word." We both laughed, but each time that I sat at the bar I would think of some obscure word that she had never heard, but could use. I gave her words like morose, obtuse, etc.

I have written newspaper columns along these same lines. I encourage people to find and use new words. And I beg them to get rid of some worn-our expressions, such as "cool, awesome, enjoy your meal."

Just monitor your daily dealings and see how often you hear those words. They are "one size fits all" and they have outlived their usefulness.

Try adding a new word to your vocabulary on occasion and limit some of the lazy language you have used to express yourself.

You will make a better impression.

Exercise and exorcise your vocabulary.

EXPERIENCE LIFE'S RITUALS

It's sometimes easier to avoid life's rituals, especially those involving death, but they must be observed.

Years back I was working on a small newspaper in a college town. There was a freak accident in a bar one night. There was a fight and bottles were broken. One piece of glass flew across the room and pictured a young woman's neck. She died.

The victim was not involved in the altercation. It was a freak accident.

I was working as a police reporter and I covered that tragic story. It saddened the entire community.

The parents of the victim (they lived in a different town) had trouble coping with the death. There was no wake or funeral service.

Exactly one year after the death I got a call from the parents asking for more information. It was obvious that they had not properly dealt with this family loss. They were still struggling with the grieving process.

I talked with morticians at the time and found this occasionally occurs. People don't like wakes or funerals so they avoid them. Those events make people feel uncomfortable.

It is important to experience these life (and death) rituals.

Funerals and memorial services are for survivors not the deceased. The process of grieving is normal, but your life can be thrown out of balance if you don't experience the proper passages.

BECOME A FILM FAN

Going to the movies is good for you. You step out of your world and into another. It's worthwhile for the temporary distraction.

You will notice that I said "going to the movies." Video rentals are not the same experience. You need to walk into a dark auditorium, watch on the big screen and focus your attention of the feature.

I don't have any stock in movie theaters, but I'm still an advocate.

Tastes vary when it come to films. Some people seek action and adventure. Others want romance. My choice is a movie with a message. In my job at various newspapers I dealt with people who were suffering and going through hard times. I go to movies for entertainment (humor is good) and an uplifting theme. I don't think there is much relaxation value in movies packed with conflict and tension, however I recognize their ability to sell tickets.

The theater experience is also very different than watching a movie at home. It is more comfortable watching from your favorite chair or couch, but many movies are made for the big screen and their impact is lost on smaller, home TVs.

The only reservation about movies is their increasing cost. Many theaters offer discounts for matinees and early showings. You get the same experience at a price that fits more budgets.

Find a way to visit a movie theater on occasion. It's a nice break.

BRING BACK THE SWITCHBOARD

Technology can cause frustration. If that's the case, we must find a way to deal with it.

Just recently I had to call the Internal Revenue Service (no one WANTS to call the IRS) and get copies of some old tax forms. I dreaded the day. I figured it would be confusing and I was right. I was transferred and put on hold three times, ended up speaking with someone in Texas and I was on the phone for 48 minutes. I timed the call and made notes for a column that I wrote for my newspaper.

You probably have a similar horror story.

The old switchboard operator/receptionist is extinct. The new way of answering phones is with machines, both at home and in businesses. Dealing with a machine is not the same as speaking to a human.

Home answering machines are convenient, but most business answering devices are annoying. They give you options to push buttons, but you are often unsure which choice to make.

You have to plan to avoid this frustration. Don't call during busy times, such as Monday mornings. Be prepared to wait. Try to get someone's direct line if that is possible. And don't get upset when things don't work. Send a letter if you can't figure out someone's phone answering system.

I predict the day is coming when businesses will advertise: "Call us and talk with a human being and not a machine." That has great appeal in this day of shifting answering responsibilities to a phone system. People want and need human contact. A sharp CEO of customer service will see the advantage of bringing back the old switchboard and some switchboard operating "Ernestines."

TRY TO MAKE A DEAL

Negotiate everything. That may not seem possible, but it is worthwhile trying.

This struck me during a recent trip to Colorado. My wife Debbi and I were shopping in Denver. We browsed a number of shops and she found a small jewelry store. I was having coffee outside and she motioned for me to come in. She found two pieces that she really liked. She asked me to pick one, but I suggested buying both.

Debbi looked up at the clerk (who she suspected was the shop owner) and asked, "Would you give me a deal if I bought both pieces?"

Without hesitation he answered, "Sure, 15 percent off the total purchase."

I was stunned. It wasn't a huge amount of money, but it was definitely worth the effort of asking for a discount. We could just as easily have purchased both pieces at full price. We walked out with a substantial savings just by asking.

That convinced me to negotiate (OK, haggle) over other prices. It never even occurred to me to ask for a deal. I learned a lesson.

At least try to negotiate everything. Sometimes it will work and keep a few more dollars in your pocketbook.

EXERCISE YOUR MIND

Our minds are challenged in our youth and then they get a long rest. They aren't pushed and tested very often in our adult years. For most people the educational process ends after course work in elementary school, high school, trade school or college.

Is that a healthy pattern?

I don't think so. It's time-consuming, costly and difficult to continue our learning, but it's worth the effort to stretch our minds.

Just recently I decided to get a real estate sales license. Several types of real estate classes are available, but I choose to go the self-study route. It felt good to be a student again. I was reminded of my college days when I was carrying my workbooks. I studied and took tests both at home in the café at Barnes & Noble bookstore. It was good to exercise my mind.

I hadn't done these kinds of "mental calisthenics" for about 30 years. The final tests for my state license were exhausting, but exhilarating when I passed. It was nice to know that my brain still worked.

How long has it been since you enrolled in a challenging course of study? Try it. Our bodies and minds both need exercise.

GET ACQUAINTED WITH THE INTERNET

Don't fight change, embrace it. Much of the consternation in our lives is caused by change. Our routines are disrupted by a change in our families, at work or in our personal situations. Whether we can control these changes is not nearly as important as being willing and able to adjust.

People regularly ask me about computers and getting involved with the Internet. My knowledge is cursory, but I'm willing to learn. My strategy is that other people with varying skills are successfully working with computers. There's no reason that I cannot learn.

Access to the Internet has opened up vast storehouses of information and knowledge. It brings the world to our desktops, but it can also bring unwanted personal contacts right into our homes. I recently wrote several editorials for my newspaper about Internet predators and a federal law prohibiting them from praying on children. A local family had been victimized when a predator posted unwanted—and sexually oriented—information on the Internet about a young girl.

This is just one example of the challenges we will be facing in the future. Should we resist these changes? Absolutely not. Adapt to them and learn. Computer introduction courses are being offered in many places, often for free. Your local public library may already be offering computer training. Don't fight this change and feel left out. Get acquainted with new technology. Other people—no smarter than you—are computer literate. You can easily adapt to this change in communications.

JOIN A GROUP AND GROW

If today's fast pace is getting you down, you may not be thinking of adding more to your schedule, but that may be just what you need.

You feel pulled in 100 different ways: work, family, home, exercise, etc. There's no time to even read the newspaper. I have heard that refrain a 100 times.

It may seem to be an unlikely suggestion, but try joining some kind of community group. The list of options is endless: service club, church group, special interest organization, etc.

Your first reaction might be doubtful. You don't need more meetings, dues, events, etc. Just the opposite might be true.

You might need the right relationships and conversations that come from community group membership. Pick a group whose schedule you can handle and give it a try. You aren't making a lifetime commitment, you are just joining to see if group participation is beneficial.

The interplay with group members may provide a welcome tonic of camaraderie and confidence. You expand your social circle and business network.

Community groups often have a specific mission that may bring you personal fulfillment, but participation is likely to bring you even more personal gain.

It may not seem like you have time to be part of a community group, but give it a whirl. You might need a new circle of friends.

USE MUSIC TO LIFT YOUR SPIRIT

Music can control your mood. Take advantage of it.

I'm not a musician, but I recognize the power of music. It can lift your spirit or make you feel depressed. Music can slow you down or spark energy and enthusiasm. Music has inspirational power.

Pick out music that can help you through the day…or night.

Many people play music in their homes and cars. Others have music playing while they work.

Like caffeine, a lively tune can invigorate you at mid-afternoon, when you need a little lift. Use music to keep the adrenaline flowing. Your music of choice might be opera, country & western or marching bands. Each person is stimulated by different kinds of music.

A song that makes you sing is better than a sugar snack or a caffeine-crammed beverage. Music is calorie- and fat-free.

The sounds that appeal to you can have a calming effect, much like a conversation with a family member or old friend.

Make music a part of your life. It gets the job done and it's not addictive.

"HUG A TREE" STILL GOOD ADVICE

It's good to interact with nature. There are many ways to accomplish this. Select something that works for you.

The admonition from the 1960s was "go hug a tree." That's still true.

An occasional walk in the woods (a park is fine if you live in the city) will do. You will be surprised how good it feels to walk on the ground. We spend so many hours at work, at home or walking in shopping malls, that it is uplifting to connect with the Earth and nature.

Perhaps you already tend your flower garden or lawn. One of my pleasures has been feeding the birds in a small feeder outside of the window by my desk at work. I fill the feeder each morning and it's a joy to watch the activity all day long. My guests are mostly sparrows with a few cardinals. Once in a while a different kind of bird arrives and it causes such a stir, even for me.

There are outstanding TV programs dealing with nature and animals. They are worth watching, but nothing beats some personal contact, even if that means visiting a zoo.

Man needs to remember that he is just one part of this big world. Interacting with animals, even if it's just your own dog or cat, is good for your balance.

TEAMMATES WILL BECOME BEST FRIENDS

Being a team player has more than the obvious value of working together toward a common goal.

You have probably been advised to "be a team player" in various phases of your life. We're told to be "part of the team" in sports, at work, in social groups, etc. Even when dining out, we strive to be part of the group so everyone is comfortable.

The value that I see in being a team player, however, is different than you imagine.

I consider myself to be fortunate to have been part of many teams in high school. My teammates became my friends, and they are still my best friends today. That's quite an acknowledgement over 40 years later.

I think there is real value in teams. That's why I encourage young people today—boys and girls—to be part of some kind of team in their school years. I believe they will form lasting friendships that they will treasure throughout the passing years. It can be sports, music, clubs, etc.

My best friends are my old teammates. We are not in constant contact, but the bond of friendship remains. I feel that I can count on them and vice versa.

Be part of a team and make friends for life.

HANG IN FOR THE LONG HAUL

Most people give up before they reach their goals.

Don't do that. Be persistent. It will pay off.

Most difficult tasks require a long commitment: losing weight, acquiring a new skill, learning a foreign language, etc.

The adage that "nothing good comes easily" is still true.

Just recently I took a course at the local junior college. The instructor said that only 25 percent of the students present would complete the class, pass the necessary test and use the state license that was the goal of taking the class.

That was surprising, but it is true of many areas of interest. People enroll in classes and quit when it gets complicated. They follow a diet, but eventually stop and gain back all of the weight they have lost.

You must be committed for the long haul to be successful. Anything stretched out over a long period gets tedious and tiring. Expect that and grit your teeth.

Don't be a quitter. Hang in there and you will reach your goals.

A LOMBARDI PEP TALK

The late Vince Lombardi, one-time coach of the Green Bay Packers, was my childhood hero. I grew up near Green Bay and I met him once or twice, but I certainly didn't know him personally.

I did, however, have great respect for him, his demeanor and his work ethic.

It's my belief that his philosophy was that hard work results in success.

I won't put words in his mouth, but I think I know enough about Lombardi to paraphrase his philosophy on life.

Football coaches and military leaders often espouse the value of striving to win.

Lombardi is often quoted and chastised for his alleged "win at all cost" philosophy. I believe that is slightly distorted.

It's my interpretation that Lombardi believed in setting your goal on winning and working relentlessly toward that goal. If you don't set out to win, you certainly won't.

"Win at all costs" indicates that you will use any means, including cheating and other improper ways, to attain victory.

I don't believe that Coach Lombardi meant that. I subscribe to his approach of hard work leading to success.

When the going gets tough, we all could use a Lombardi pep talk.

DON'T DIET, CHANGE YOUR LIFE

The word diet has multiple interpretations. Its dictionary meaning is long, but can generally be applied to the foods that a person eats most often.

Most people use the term "diet" to describe a change in their eating routines. For example, "I'm on a diet to lose 20 pounds." In my opinion a "diet" is temporary and won't work.

You need to make lifestyle changes.

Weight loss is a goal for a large number of people. There are numerous diets and weight loss programs on the market.

Some work, some don't. Weight loss is a target for many people whose lives are out of whack. They believe that losing excess pounds will bring balance into their lives. I tend to agree. But I don't advocate a diet. I believe you have to modify your lifestyle. I did that 30 years ago when I weighed over 300 pounds.

I never saw my weight loss program as a "diet." I started walking and exercising to burn up calories. I made a conscious effort to eat in moderation. I reduced sugars, fats and other pound producers. In the 1970s there were far fewer healthier foods on the market than today.

I had to improvise. I ate a lot of plain baked potatoes. I ate a lot of dry bread. I ate many of the foods I liked, but in reduced quantities. I cut out desserts. I took great pleasure in turning down treats like cake, cookies, etc. I took control of my eating patterns, but I never considered my plan a diet.

And it worked for me. I was able to lose over 100 pounds and have kept them off.

If losing weight is your goal, call you plan a lifestyle change and not a diet. You will then see this change as permanent and not a temporary fix.

RELIGION PLAYS VITAL ROLE

Many people will say your life is out of whack if you are not spiritual. I tend to agree.

Religion is of utmost importance to a large number of people.

Some people feel a void if they are not involved with spiritual activities.

Others get great strength from practicing religion.

I am a Christian, but I will not tell others to join a certain religion or avoid others. I feel there is great value in being part of any religion.

People may debate specific doctrines, but I think the benefit derived from a religious life is teaching people the proper way to live. Respect, love, consideration and high morals are among the tenets of spiritual life.

I am a believer that faith in God and practicing religion are necessary to keep balance in your life.

INTROSPECTION PAYS OFF

My life got out of whack when I went through a divorce. I'm sure that's the case with most people who go through similar, life-altering experiences.

I learned a lot, especially about myself.

I gave considerable thought to what is important to me as far as a relationship with a spouse. I had never done that before.

I would not recommend this trauma to force you to think about your priorities, but it works. I would suggest sitting down and practicing some introspection on a regular basis, regardless of your marital status. You might find you are very happy with your current situation or you might find you have to make changes.

In my case, I found that what I valued was companionship and a physical relationship. That's probably pretty normal, but I never clearly identified those needs.

Each person is different. You might discover other things are important to you, such as financial security, etc. Figure out what you value and work toward those goals.

COMPLAINING ONLY COMPOUNDS PROBLEMS

It's my contention that complaining only compounds your problems. Try to avoid being a complainer. People tire easily of others who grouse all of the time. And there are a lot of those people.

Every time you talk with complainers, they have some sort of malady or trouble. These negative conversations can be draining on you. Pretty soon you become sour on the world.

Don't fall into that trap. Try to find a silver lining in your clouds and more people will enjoy being around you.

On one Thanksgiving Day I came down with a cold. I had all of the usual aches and pains. When that happens, I try not to let this temporary setback throw me off course. I was fortunate that this illness came at the end of a week when I had some extra time on the weekend to rest and recuperate.

My wife Debbi marveled at my outlook. She said most people would moan and curse their bad luck. She was amazed I could be positive about being sick.

Problems—such as illness or other personal troubles—are upsetting, but there is usually a positive path away from tribulation.

I think that complaining only adds to your discomfort and it alienates people around you. Try taking the high road and ignoring little aches and pains. You will move away from your problems faster and other people will appreciate your upbeat attitude.

DON'T WORRY ABOUT PLEASING OTHER PEOPLE

Don't worry about what other people think. A lot of people are too concerned about what other people think about them. They worry that they won't be accepted because of their actions or words. They feel awkward because of their clothes or other material possessions.

People shouldn't worry about meeting the standards of other people.

In other words, develop "thicker skin." Don't be concerned that others may be talking about you. Don't live your life seeking the approval of others.

I like to use the comparison of people living in other parts of the world: For example, will anyone in Europe know or care that you flubbed a couple of times during a speech or business meeting? Will anyone in Africa give a second thought that you shop at Wal-Mart instead of Nieman-Marcus?

This is definitely easier said than done, but the approval of others is not all that important.

A few years ago I found out this lesson the hard way. I make my living writing editorials and columns for a newspaper. A local teachers' union was involved in difficult contract negotiations. I wrote a column questioning the need to give big pay raises to the teachers.

The teachers' union representing the local high school district was livid. They lit up the switchboard at the newspaper with complaints. Eighty subscribers quit the newspaper because of my column. We published 100 letters to the editor complaining about my stance on this issue. The editors talked with disgruntled customers for nearly two weeks. My newspaper was medium sized (about 50,000 subscribers) so this was a major disruption.

My picture was put in the center of a target and posted around the school buildings. People openly expressed hatred toward me.

It was an uncomfortable time, but I learned a lot. I discovered that—even in the face of controversy—I couldn't be concerned about what other people think.

I earned a paycheck expressing my opinion so that situation may be different than yours, but I believe the same advice applies: don't worry about what other people think.

MAKE HELPING PEOPLE YOUR GOAL

One of the surest ways to be happy is to make other people happy.

That may not seem like the correct equation to produce happiness, but it works.

Go out of your way to help people, organizations and your community. Make helping your goal and you will find personal happiness.

Try helping some local fund-raising effort. Try helping at your local hospital, church or other service agency. Shop around to find what appeals to you, then make it your intention to make those people happy. You will be shocked at the results. The more you make other people happy, the better you feel.

I see lonely and unhappy people all of the time. One of the best examples is our talented senior citizen population. There is one case that sticks in my mind. An energetic and outgoing man retired from his job. Shortly after that, his wife died. He had so much to offer to society, yet he spent his days at the local off-track betting parlor. He didn't drink or gamble a lot, but gambling was a way to spend his afternoons.

He could just have easily spent a few afternoons every week helping others. He had a great personality and always wore a smile, but I don't believe he was happy. He was just going through the motions. I am convinced he would have been much happier if he had tried to make other people happy. He had that capability, but he chose to just fritter away his days.

Many senior citizens are healthy and full of energy today. I feel this is one natural resource that is untapped in most communities. The entire community would gain and the givers would also be happy.

CUT BACK ON CHORES, OBLIGATIONS

Avoid as much stress as possible. This is particularly helpful late in the year, from Thanksgiving to Christmas.

You see signs of stress spilling out all over during the final weeks of the holiday shopping season: People are arguing with checkout clerks, shoppers wear frenzied looks, drivers cut off other motorists for parking spaces, etc.

People simply have too much to do during the holiday rush.

If you have found yourself doing more, but enjoying it less, it's time to cut back, whatever time of year.

During the holidays, for example, decorate less, don't send Christmas cards, skip some holiday parties or find other ways to cut back or reduce your chores and obligations.

Less is definitely more when it comes to stress. Less stress translates to a better life.

DON'T LET A JOB DOMINATE YOUR LIFE

For about five years I was editor of a daily newspaper in northern Illinois. This paper was located in a small town with a university just west of Chicago. The school had a journalism department, where I recruited my reporters.

These were all rookie journalists, who fit in nicely with my operation, which offered low pay. The newcomers would work for me a year or so, get some experience and then move on to bigger newspapers, with better pay.

I had a staff of a dozen, and I usually had to fill as many as six vacancies during the course of a year. The reporters barely learned the ropes, before they moved on.

The enthusiasm that most of these reporters brought to their first "real" job was interesting to observe. They worked long hours, despite the low pay.

They would get so wrapped up in their jobs, that they would lose track of everything else. I would counsel them: make sure your job revolves around your life and not vice versa.

People who let their work control their lives often burn out or turn into bitter employees who hate their jobs.

A job is just one component of a life. In my field of journalism—and I'm sure many other occupations—people can get so involved in their work that they block out everything else, family members, home life, recreations, etc.

Get a job you like, but don't get to like your job too much.

A BAD MOOD ALL YEAR LONG

A short time ago I was leaving a bookstore and three young people were standing on the sidewalk talking. I walked by and overhead one young woman say in an exasperated voice: "Everybody's in a bad mood this year."

I had to chuckle. Everybody. Bad mood. THIS YEAR.

I guess that summed up this young woman's observation of the world around her.

Perhaps you have had the same thought. Does it seem that everyone is unhappy? Maybe some of us need an attitude adjustment.

I observe a lot of sour people. I didn't realize how many until I ran across an especially cheerful and bouncy waitress. Her mood was a stark contrast to the other waitresses with long faces.

The people with smiles on their faces and cheery attitudes have the same amount of problems as the rest of us. They just choose to be happy.

That's a good example for all of us. Consider how you interact with other people on a daily basis. Do other people think you have been in a bad mood this entire year?

NEVER THINK THAT YOU ARE BETTER

The worst personality flaw is not respecting others.

You must have the highest consideration for other people, or it will show.

You must believe that all people are equal, or it will show.

Be assured that no one is any better or any less important than you. Don't look down your nose at other people or stand in awe of other people. We are all the same.

Start each day with that on your mind and you will be better off. Social status, wealth, accomplishments, etc. are worldly possessions. Some of us have less, some of us have more.

It's my contention that the worst personality flaw is thinking you are better than the next person. You can sense this flaw in people immediately. For example, a person doesn't listen to you, doesn't look you in the eye or doesn't acknowledge your presence. Those are some telltale signs. You meet people like this all of the time.

They think they are better than you. That's a major mistake. The basic premise that we are all created equal is still the guiding principle. Don't ever feel that you are any less or any better than anyone else.

TAKE DELIGHT IN YOUR SELF-CONTROL

Take great pleasure in your self-control. We all have problems and those require some discipline.

Don't wallow in self-pity when you have to deny yourself something, take pleasure that you have will power.

Years ago I struggled with a severe weight problem. I was determined to lose weight and I started taking the necessary steps to reduce my calories and increase my exercise.

I was working at a small newspaper in Wisconsin at the time. Like other small businesses, there were office birthdays and other celebrations. Fellow workers would bring in boxes of candy and pastries on these occasions.

I was trying to cut my fats and calories so these treats were great temptations.

I enjoyed the fact that I could turn them down. I would think to myself, "I can't eat this candy or donut like other people. I have to be strong in this situation." I would politely turn down these sweets and instead ask for another cup of coffer or diet beverage. I knew that self-denial was necessary to lose weight. And I would smile to myself, "I did it. I am pleased that I turned down something that isn't good for me."

This is a good exercise. Don't just practice self-control, relish it and be proud of yourself.

EXPECT TO HAVE GOOD LUCK

Call it eternal optimism, but I encourage people to expect good luck.

It's like the old saying about being careful what you ask for, you may get what you seek.

I believe there is a great value in dreaming, having a vision and expecting good things to happen.

Some days that may seem highly unlikely. The car won't start, you have an argument at home or trouble at work. It's one of THOSE days. Fight it off.

Expect your next day to be better. Take some consolation in knowing that everyone has problems. Even the most successful, seemingly content and accomplished people have bad days.

The key is to look past those troubles. Don't dwell on difficulties.

Expect that something good is going to happen to you in the near future. That will bolster your spirit.

It may be something small like receiving a compliment or running across something that you need and it's on sale. It might be something large like a pay raise or even winning a prize in a drawing.

Expect good things to happen. And they will.

DON'T GET YOUR TAIL TANGLED

One of my mother's favorite phrases was "don't get your tail in a knot."

It's the perfect advice for living in today's world.

Don't get too excited and worked up about anything.

I don't remember my mother talking about stress or ways to relieve it. She died in the 1980s, before pressure and stress became buzz words.

She recognized, however, when people were having trouble dealing with worldly problems. Their anxiety was high. They couldn't cope. Whether it was trouble at home, work, school or church, she admonished them: "Don't get your tail in a knot."

Remember that phrase when you are having difficulties. It will make you smile and help you put your problem in perspective.

DEVELOP SOME INNER PEACE

Early in the 1980s I had the chance to visit Rome and see the Pope. What amazed me most was his serenity. He seemed to have inner peace.

He went into the large crowd and touched hundreds—if not thousands—of people. He moved slowly and deliberately. He did not seem affected by the huge throng of well-wishers.

And this was only a couple of years after he had been shot.

He remained calm despite all of the hubbub around him.

I think that's a good lesson for all of us.

Don't get distracted by the swirl of activities around you. People in high places seem to have this capability. There's no reason we all can't stay calm in the daily din.

Practice having inner peace. When the volume and pace increase in your regular activities, pause and remember the importance of being calm on the inside. You may not always be able to do that, but try.

Think about how the Pope and other people in high places have a calm air surrounding them. You can also have inner peace.

HELP THE "RUDYS" OF THE WORLD

The United States has always been the land of the "little guy." This nation was founded on the notion that the underdog can triumph.

We relish stories about "Davids" defeating "Goliaths."

In fact, we are prone to help "little guys" overcome adversity.

We love that "can do" spirit in sports teams, politicians and our fellow man.

My current home is in Joliet, Illinois, which is also the home of "Rudy," the gritty and determined football player who persevered and finally got into a game for the University of Notre Dame team.

Rudy is an inspiring story that was made into a movie. He even had to fight to get his story onto the big screen. And now Rudy has made a career of telling his story in public appearances.

We are moved by Rudy's persistence and "never quit" attitude. We cheer on the Rudys of the world and we are even willing to help them.

The perfect example of this phenomenon is the former pro wrestler who was elected governor of Minnesota. Jesse "The Body" Ventura is no "little guy" in the literal sense, but in the figurative sense he defeated the establishment. And I'll bet all of the people who voted for Ventura felt satisfaction that they helped elect an "outsider."

Help a "little guy" once in a while and you will feel better, too.

HAVE CLASS LIKE TONY BENNETT

Keep your chin up. That's a cliché, but it's still true. Some days the world weighs pretty heavy, but it's important to push forward with dignity and class.

You think you have tough times? Think back to the days when President Clinton was facing an impeachment debate in the House of Representatives while simultaneously brokering peace in the Middle East and ordering air strikes against Iraq. Think about President Bush after Sept. 11 and what was going through his mind.

It's important for all of us to have class in the face of adversity. You will lose some battles, but try hard to keep your dignity in all situations. People will forget your victories and defeats, but they will remember that you were a person with class.

I think of singer Tony Bennett. His career extended over decades and I'm sure there must have been low points, but he has always been graceful. People will remember his sophistication, just like they will remember yours.

BEST SALES TOOL IS A COMPLIMENT

Kill them with kindness. That may sound like an over-simplification, but people still want to be praised and hear kind words.

Kindness is the best sales tool ever.

People remember and respond when you compliment or comment on something positive about them.

Parents glow when someone sees their family photos and comments about a good-looking family.

People are pleased when someone praises their attire or hairstyle.

Most people are even happy when someone notices that they smile a lot.

Always look for something good to say about the people you meet. Your compliment will be remembered.

Don't be phony about it, but find something that is praise-worthy.

It's my belief that the best salesmen and saleswomen are those who notice the little things and comment on them. There are many competent sales people, but the most successful ones will develop a habit of using kind and sincere words.

CLARIFY YOUR PRIORITIES

What things in life are important to you? And—almost as important—what things are not important?

Have you ever ranked what is most essential to your happiness and well-being?

Is your family at the top of your priorities? How about your friends? Does your religious belief get the highest billing? And how about your health?

Make a list of your priorities. It won't be as long as you think.

This list helps you define where you want to place your emphasis and attention. What is most important, what is next, etc?

The usual topics are faith, health, family, friends, work, etc. You can also include possessions such as home, car, wardrobe, hobbies and so on.

Put this list in writing and then commit it to memory so you carry it along with you.

Review your priorities regularly to see if you are spending time on things that are important to you or wasting time on topics that are insignificant.

DRESS UP, DON'T DRESS DOWN

You can't fool all of the people all of the time, but you can fool some just by dressing correctly.

Don't dress down to the acceptable level where you work. Dress up.

That makes you look impressive and feel confident. Always pick your best attire possible for work and other responsibilities.

Don't be uncaring about how you appear.

Who is going to get the better response; a man or woman in sharp looking clothes, or someone in jeans and a sloppy sweatshirt?

The advice to "dress for success" still holds true.

Attractive clothes have two advantages: First, other people assume you have some status, which might get special treatment for you. Second, you stand out in a crowd when all other things are equal.

This tip applies to all occupations, whether you work in the back of a kitchen or sit in an obscure cubicle. Dress for the part that you want in life's play.

Don't let the clothes of your colleagues dictate how you will dress. Wear the best outfit you have each day. Dress codes have been relaxed in most work places. Casual is in; dressy is out.

Don't let that dictate your clothes or personal hygiene. Your over-all image will be enhanced by a nice appearance.

SEE THE FUTURE IN A RETIREMENT HOME

Do you want to develop a new appreciation of life? Visit a nursing home.

A short time ago I was invited to tour a large retirement home in my hometown. I was going to write a column on this facility so I received a complete tour, especially designed for a member of the press.

I met almost every resident of this home. Many of the residents recognized me from the newspaper so I was treated like a celebrity. I greeted and chatted with many. The tour took all afternoon.

It was worth every minute. Some residents were feeble and some hard of hearing, but most were wearing smiles.

You see the world differently through the eyes of nursing home residents. They love camaraderie and simple things. A flower or a cookie brings such pleasure. They have strong faith and appreciate time more than people in the working world. It's quiet in their hallways; the hubbub of daily life that busy people abhor has disappeared.

A retirement home is a glimpse of what is ahead in your world. It's not all bad, but it makes you take a second look at everything you are doing. A nursing home is both a blast from the past and a glimpse of your future.

PLOP, PLOP, FIZZ, FIZZ
IT'S A RELIEF LOOKING FOR A NEW JOB

One of the most upsetting parts of life is having a job that makes you unhappy.

If that's your situation, it's time for a change. Many people labor in jobs that they dislike.

The culture of the work place is changing. Workers no longer expect to stay with one employer for their entire careers. Changing jobs is inevitable in today's marketplace.

Expect to move on and don't wait if you don't enjoy your work. In fact, just making the decision to start looking for a new job will make you feel better.

You don't have to tell anyone you are looking for another job. That can be your little secret. Organize your job hunt and get started. Commit yourself to leaving your present job and finding something new.

And surprisingly, the job you hate now may not seem as bad once you have committed to change. Be patient. It will take time to find a new job, but a burden will be lifted from your shoulders once you are dedicated to moving on.

PETS ARE GREAT PALS

Over the years I have written stories for my newspaper on a number of events in schools and nursing homes. One of the best is when animals are brought in to visit the children or the senior citizens. The love and affection flows freely.

The animals love the attention and the kids and elderly love to shower it on dogs, cats and other creatures.

Bring an animal into your life if you want companionship. A dog or cat will bring you great pleasure and take your mind off of any troubles.

For two decades I worked with a grizzled newspaper writer. He loved guns, John Wayne and action movies. He was gruff from years of covering police news and tragic events, but he had a big heart. He changed a lot when a kitten entered his life. He devoted lots of time to entertaining this tiny feline and he received lots of affection in return. You will experience the same feelings.

A pet—even a goldfish—can bring you companionship and satisfaction.

You make a pal when you take in a pet.

PREPARE A DAILY 'RUN LIST'

Each evening I take a note card and list the tasks and errands that I need to accomplish the next day. I find this is especially helpful in remembering what has to be done and focusing on specific chores.

I list my meetings, personal chores and my regular goals such as writing as soon as I get into work. In the newspaper business, this "To Do" list is called a manifest or a "run sheet." It's a list of what articles are planned for the paper on a given day.

This personal list is tucked into my shirt pocket and I review it throughout the day. I find that it helps me avoid having too many tasks and not enough time at the end of the day. I work on that list all day long. Without the list I would invariably forget to do something and feel frustrated that I had to run an errand in the evening.

It also brings satisfaction at the end of the day when all of the chores are crossed off and it's time for a little relaxation.

DON'T WAIT IN LONG LINES FOR ANYTHING

There have been many books written about simplifying our lives. I agree with them. We have too many complications.

This wonderful world with rapid technology and more information than we can handle is confusing and hard to navigate.

We are responsible for some of these complications, but there are factors we can control.

Don't take on everything that comes down the road. For example, you want to go to a concert or sporting event, but you don't want the stress of standing in line or dialing the phone for hours to get tickets. Simply skip that event and reduce your anticipated stress. If you feel unhappy about that, buy a CD or book as a replacement.

I collected autographs for years, but I became disenchanted when businesses started selling them and shows were arranged with long lines of people paying to get the signatures of celebrities.

I wonder about the value of anything that requires us to stand in long lines. I won't do that anymore. Find an alternative and avoid the stress.

EVEN OUR GAMES ARE COMPLICATED

When I was growing up we had a foreign exchange teacher stay in our home for a few weeks. She was a young woman from Sweden. She was attractive and interested in all aspects of American culture.

I was in high school at the time and it was obvious that the male teachers were more than willing to accommodate her desire to learn about the United States.

One day my parents were giving this woman a tour of our small town in central Wisconsin. It was fall and the Green Bay Packer game was on the radio.

She asked me to explain football. Just try explaining football—or any other game—to someone who has no knowledge of sports. Nothing makes sense. Why are there 11 players on a team? Why do you get six points for a touchdown? And what's a touchdown?

You get the point. It's a challenge to explain the basics of sports games.

The whole point of this vignette is to illustrate the complexity of today's world. Even the games we play are complicated.

Don't let that complexity get you down. Learn about some activities, but don't expect to be an expert on many things. And—just for a laugh—try explaining your favorite sport to someone who knows nothing about it.

BE A FRIEND WITH YOUR CUSTOMERS

One of the best ways to be successful and bring satisfaction to your life is to make more friends. Expand your social circle.

That may sound elementary, but it's not necessarily easy.

This is extremely important in your work. Whatever your occupation, make friends with you customers and clients.

Every job has some form of "customer service." Make your "customer service" different than all others. Become friends with your "customers."

Be courteous, professional and out-going. Treat your customers like they are your fiends.

People act differently when the customers they are serving are friends and not strangers. Friends get special treatment, consideration and follow-up. Strangers are treated with indifference.

It may take a little more time to be sociable and become friends with your customers, but it will be well worth the effort.

Don't you feel better about dealing with friends at the bank, department store or insurance company? Wouldn't you rather deal with a friend than a stranger?

It's my belief that businesses in the future will need to be more "friendly." Technology has taken the human element out of doing business. Businesses in the future will be advertising that they are customer-friendly and you deal with human beings and not computers.

Get ahead of that game. Make friends with all people who you meet. Your reward will be great.

FIND A SOUNDING BOARD FOR PROBLEMS

We all have problems to sort out. How we handle them determines how quickly and completely they are resolved.

The best thing I can suggest is to find somebody who will listen to your problem.

I'm not good at this. I tend to mull over troubles in my mind before I talk about them to anyone else. I think it's better to do this the opposite way. Talk to someone else before you spend too much time considering options for your problems.

In this regard, it's good to have a relative or friend who you trust and whose opinion you respect.

When the problems get thick, go to your "sounding board" and verbalize what's bothering you. Sometimes just saying things out loud puts them in different perspective. And you might get a good suggestion from your "sounding board." I know that works with me. When I first started going through a divorce, I would talk endlessly with my golfing buddy. He had divorce experience so he understood my problems and had suggestions.

If you don't want to share these troubles with a friend or relative, try professional help.

Many employers offer professional counseling on a variety of issues as part of their benefits package. Take advantage of that.

BECOME A "FAN" OF SOMETHING NEW

Some people have plates that are too full. Some people have empty plates. There's probably a happy medium, but this essay is aimed at people who have time on their hands.

In many instances, those folks are elderly and they spend a lot of time at home.

They need to develop an interest in something that is readily available and inexpensive.

They need to become "fans." They need to take a special interest in something and spend time pursuing that subject. Being a "fan" is usually associated with sports, but it can apply to any other interest.

People can be "fans" of the food channel on cable, or even the weather channel. They might increase their attention to music or travel. More and more interests—even wrestling—are accommodated on TV. If you can't get cable service, try a satellite dish. If that doesn't work, subscribe to magazines, go to bookstores for niche publications.

The idea is to get interested in something new to you.

It will take your mind off of your troubles and give you something to talk about. You are likely to make new friends.

FIND A HIDING PLACE

This suggestion applies whether you are boss or employee, child or parent, married or single, etc.

You need to find a hiding place.

You need to have a spot where you can escape for a few minutes by yourself.

The point is that you go there by yourself to collect your thoughts.

I did this when I worked as a news editor and we passed our final deadline for that day's edition. There were few places in our newspaper building to get away for a few minutes so I would walk back by the loading dock to escape the telephone and clamoring voices. A couple of minutes of tranquility and I was ready to go back to work.

Parents with kids in the house know about this need to escape. Even a cup of tea or coffee away from home will help settle your nerves.

Find a hiding place.

Stop on your way home from work for a few minutes of solitude. It might help keep your life from getting out of whack.

WALK AWAY FROM TROUBLE

An admonition that I learned in the business world also applies to personal problems: Walk away, don't burn bridges.

When conflict arises and you need to get out of a bad situation, simply separate yourself from the circumstances as best you can.

Many people are bitter, carry grudges or they want revenge. It's not worth the effort.

That advice works in the business world and elsewhere.

You may have hard feelings after suffering some kind of "defeat" at work, such as being fired or being forced to change jobs. In most cases, it's better to move on with your life and not look back.

It's the same in your personal life. You are sure to have some tough times with your friends, your mate or your relatives. You will have to deal with the deaths of others and other difficulties such as divorce. These situations are all part of living. Do your best to adjust and then move on with your life.

Some people struggle with these situations for long periods. They want to "pay back" someone for these tough times. They harbor hard feelings. Don't do that.

Seeking revenge only drains your energy. Walk away and don't burn bridges.

HAVE REASONABLE EXPECTATIONS

Sometimes we are responsible for our own disappointments. Guard against that.

We set our goals too high or we anticipate success and good fortune that are unlikely to occur.

We must be realistic about all of our expectations. For example, have you ever anticipated a fantastic dinner at your favorite restaurant and it turned out to be a disaster? Have you hoped for a work promotion when you knew that many other employees were much better qualified? The list of those disappointments goes on and on.

It is important to dream and set goals, but keep things in perspective. Have realistic expectations.

I always hope for the best, but I try to be honest about my chances. I know that a lot of things can mess up the works. Keep that in mind.

You will have fewer disappointments when you have realistic expectations.

THE WORLD WON'T END

The kids are sick, the car won't start, an unexpected bill arrives and you are behind on a project at work. You feel like you are carrying the weight of the world. Everything is going bad.

One consoling thought to keep in the back of your mind is: "the world won't end."

Repeat that when the suction of problems is pulling you down: "the world won't end."

Regardless of how many troubles are bothering you, the rest of the world goes on. And so will you and your life.

I have visited numerous crime scenes over the years while covering the police beat. Moments after a violent act has occurred—including murder—the location returns to normal. You can't ell that a crime was committed.

That's the same way it will work with you. Most situations and the circumstances surrounding them will vanish quickly and the world continues.

This is not to say that you should ignore deadlines and other obligations, but most big problems become little memories after a short time.

Consider your options and do the best you can with all difficulties, but remember that no matter what happens: "the world won't end."

CAREFULLY CONSIDER LEGAL RECOURSE

People are clogging the courts with lawsuits. It's my belief that all of those suits are throwing too many lives out of whack.

Sometime during the course of your life you will be given the option of filing a lawsuit against someone or some business.

Please carefully consider that. Getting involved in a suit is a long process and it causes a lot of stress.

The usual reward is financial gain, but it won't come without considerable anxiety. A cash carrot may entice you, but you need to consider the downside of a long, drawn-out battle that you may not win.

This is not to say you shouldn't consider legal action if you are wronged, but weigh all alternatives before agreeing to be part of a suit.

People watch too many TV shows about the courts and lawyers. We see people suits with wild claims. I'm no lawyer and I would never even suggest legal advice, but I would ask you to be careful if you are considering a lawsuit.

"WEIGH YOUR WORDS"

Years ago I worked on the news desk of my newspaper and our pages were assembled in the back shop.

I got to know many of the workers in the back shop. We joked back and forth and shared views on the world.

Sometimes things would be serious. One man in particular would wave his index finger and admonish me to "weigh your words." A literal translation of that phrase: be careful what you say.

That's good advice.

I urge people to be friendly, wear a smile and be out-going, but be cautious about being too chatty. Sometimes your words and comments can come back to haunt you.

The man in our back shop was right on the mark with "weigh your words." An off-hand comment can be hurtful or obligate you to live up to your promises.

There are occasions when it is better just to listen and keep comments to ourselves.

We have all said things that we regretted later. Weigh your words.

NEW YEAR'S BAD FOR RESOLUTIONS

New Year's Day is the usual time for resolutions. A lot of public attention is paid to people resolving to change their lives in some way. You know the usual list: lose weight, add exercise, quit smoking, etc.

I don't know if there are statistics on New Year's resolutions, but I bet very few are kept.

The stumbling block is the date. You can't wait for New Year's Day to make a change.

If you want to make a change in your life, do it today. Don't wait until tomorrow or New Year's Day. Once you resolve in your mind to make a change, you need to begin immediately. If you pick a date in the future, you will not make the change. If you decide to wait for a while, you have NOT decided to make the change.

New Year's Day is not a magical date for resolutions. Any day is better. New Year's Day is the worst.

Make this resolution: If you want to make a change in your life and you build in any sort of delay, your resolution is likely to fail. If you resolve to change, do it immediately. You cannot afford to wait until tomorrow.

A SURPRISE ENDING

This book has a surprise ending.

Don't even try to use all of the suggestions in this book.

Pick a few that interest you. Pick a few that you can manage.

Here are nearly 100 ideas in this book. That's a lot to swallow. Choose a few and try to incorporate them into your life.

This book is not a manual for overhauling your life. It's an outline for tinkering to make things better.

You probably didn't expect to read this particular advice in the final chapter. A lot of authors want you to use their entire plan.

I'm the opposite. I say pick and choose. Keep this book on your bed stand and review it periodically. Find an idea that will help you improve your life.

Is your life out of whack?

One of the ideas in this book might help.

And thanks for reading.

0-595-21804-0